Mitchell

by Murray Ogilvie

Lang**Syne**

PUBLISHING

WRITING *to* REMEMBER

Lang**Syne**

PUBLISHING

WRITING *to* REMEMBER

79 Main Street, Newtongrange,
Midlothian EH22 4NA
Tel: 0131 344 0414   Fax: 0845 075 6085
E-mail: info@lang-syne.co.uk
www.langsyneshop.co.uk

Design by Dorothy Meikle
Printed by Ricoh Print Scotland
© Lang Syne Publishers Ltd 2015

ISBN 978-1-85217-287-9

Mitchell

MOTTO:
In deo spes
(There is hope in God).

ASSOCIATED NAMES:
Mechel
Meitchel
Michell
Michill
Mitchell
Mitchol
Mitschael
Mitsschal
Mittchel
Mychell
Mytchell

*Echoes of a far distant past
can still be found in most names*

Chapter one:

Origins of Scottish surnames

by George Forbes

It all began with the Normans.

For it was they who introduced surnames into common usage more than a thousand years ago, initially based on the title of their estates, local villages and chateaux in France to distinguish and identify these landholdings, usually acquired at the point of a bloodstained sword.

Such grand descriptions also helped enhance the prestige of these arrogant warlords and generally glorify their lofty positions high above the humble serfs slaving away below in the pecking order who only had single names, often with Biblical connotations as in Pierre and Jacques.

The only descriptive distinctions among this peasantry concerned their occupations, like Pierre the swineherd or Jacques the ferryman.

The Normans themselves were originally Vikings (or Northmen) who raided, colonised and eventually settled down around the French coastline.

They had sailed up the Seine in their long-boats in 900AD under their ferocious leader Rollo and ruled the roost in north east France before sailing over to conquer England, bringing their relatively new tradition of having surnames with them.

It took another hundred years for the Normans to percolate northwards and surnames did not begin to appear in Scotland until the thirteenth century.

These adventurous knights brought an aura of chivalry with them and it was said no damsel of any distinction would marry a man unless he had at least two names.

The family names included that of Scotland's great hero Robert De Brus and his compatriots were warriors from families like the De Morevils, De Umphravils, De Berkelais, De Quincis, De Viponts and De Vaux.

As the knights settled the boundaries of

their vast estates, they took territorial names, as in Hamilton, Moray, Crawford, Cunningham, Dunbar, Ross, Wemyss, Dundas, Galloway, Renfrew, Greenhill, Hazelwood, Sandylands and Church-hill.

Other names, though not with any obvious geographical or topographical features, nevertheless derived from ancient parishes like Douglas, Forbes, Dalyell and Guthrie.

Other surnames were coined in connection with occupations, castles or legendary deeds. Stuart originated in the word steward, a prestigious post which was an integral part of any large medieval household. The same applied to Cooks, Chamberlains, Constables and Porters.

Borders towns and forts – needed in areas like the Debateable Lands which were constantly fought over by feuding local families – had their own distinctive names; and it was often from them that the resident groups took their communal titles, as in the Grahams of Annandale, the Elliots and Armstrongs of the East Marches, the Scotts and Kerrs of Teviotdale and Eskdale.

Even physical attributes crept into surnames, as in Small, Little and More (the latter being 'beg' in Gaelic), Long or Lang, Stark, Stout, Strong or Strang and even Jolly.

Mieklejohns would have had the strength of several men, while Littlejohn was named after the legendary sidekick of Robin Hood.

Colours got into the act with Black, White, Grey, Brown and Green (Red developed into Reid, Ruddy or Ruddiman). Blue was rare and nobody ever wanted to be associated with yellow.

Pompous worthies took the name Wiseman, Goodman and Goodall.

Words intimating the sons of leading figures were soon affiliated into the language as in Johnson, Adamson, Richardson and Thomson, while the Norman equivalent of Fitz (from the French-Latin 'filius' meaning 'son') cropped up in Fitzmaurice and Fitzgerald.

The prefix 'Mac' was 'son of' in Gaelic and clans often originated with occupations – as in MacNab being sons of the Abbot, MacPherson and MacVicar being sons of the minister and MacIntosh being sons of the chief.

The church's influence could be found in the names Kirk, Clerk, Clarke, Bishop, Friar and Monk. Proctor came from a church official, Singer and Sangster from choristers, Gilchrist and Gillies from Christ's servant, Mitchell, Gilmory and Gilmour from servants of St Michael and Mary, Malcolm from a servant of Columba and Gillespie from a bishop's servant.

The rudimentary medical profession was represented by Barber (a trade which also once included dentistry and surgery) as well as Leech or Leitch.

Businessmen produced Merchants, Mercers, Monypennies, Chapmans, Sellers and Scales, while down at the old village watermill the names that cropped up included Miller, Walker and Fuller.

Other self explanatory trades included Coopers, Brands, Barkers, Tanners, Skinners, Brewsters and Brewers, Tailors, Saddlers, Wrights, Cartwrights, Smiths, Harpers, Joiners, Sawyers, Masons and Plumbers.

Even the scenery was utilised as in Craig, Moor, Hill, Glen, Wood and Forrest.

Rank, whether high or low, took its place with Laird, Barron, Knight, Tennant, Farmer, Husband, Granger, Grieve, Shepherd, Shearer and Fletcher.

The hunt and the chase supplied Hunter, Falconer, Fowler, Fox, Forrester, Archer and Spearman.

The renowned medieval historian Froissart, who eulogised about the romantic deeds of chivalry (and who condemned Scotland as being a poverty stricken wasteland), once sniffily dismissed the peasantry of his native France as the jacquerie (or the jacques-without-names) but it was these same humble folk who ended up over-throwing the arrogant aristocracy.

In the olden days, only the blueblooded knights of antiquity were entitled to full, proper names, both Christian and surnames, but with the passing of time and a more egalitarian, less feudal atmosphere, more respectful and worthy titles spread throughout the populace as a whole.

Echoes of a far distant past can still be found in most names and they can be borne with pride in commemoration of past generations who fought and toiled in some capacity or other to make our nation what it now is, for good or ill.

Chapter two:

The blood is strong

The name Mitchell is derived from the Hebrew name Michael, which means 'who is like God'. The nature of its introduction to Scotland is obscure. The most popular view is that was brought by the Normans after William the Conqueror's invasion of England in 1066. However, the name Michael was popular much earlier than that, earlier even than Roman times and it would be remarkable if it didn't exist in Scotland long before the French arrived.

Through time the name evolved from Michell via Mitsell, Mitschell, Mytschell to Mitchell, but not necessarily in that order. For example, Michell and Mitsell were being used in the fifteenth century. In the sixteenth century we find a record of Andro Mitschell listed in the Barony of Carnwath, Lanarkshire in 1544 and a John Mytschell living in Langside, near Glasgow in 1555. However, in 1611 Thomas Michell owned lands at Muirtoune, Morayshire. By the following century these older versions were on the way out and Mitchell was a common name. Of the fifteenth century Mitchells one, John Mitsell, had land in Glasgow in 1496. The other, John Michell, played an important role in a major episode in Scottish history.

James IV of Scotland became king on the death of his father, who was killed at the Battle of Sauchieburn in 1488. The rebels rose against him because James was an unpopular and ineffective monarch owing to an unwillingness to administer justice fairly, a policy of pursuing alliance with England and a disastrous relationship with nearly all his extended family. He also wanted his younger son to succeed him on the Scottish throne. James the IV, the oldest son, supported the uprising and was crowned king when it was successful. The following year he attacked Lord Darnley, the Earl of Lennox, who had been plotting against him. In July 1489 the King's army, with James leading from the front, laid siege to Darnley's stronghold, Dumbarton Castle. Despite having heavy artillery at his disposal, including Mons Meg from Edinburgh, which could fire cannon balls weighing nearly 400lbs each, Dumbarton could not be breached. James almost gave up but he tried one last time in September and on this occasion, the attack, allied to a siege, led to a surrender. But not before the Earl of Lennox negotiated a full pardon on charges of treason. As part of that deal John Michell, who had led the defence of the castle, was also rewarded.

One Mitchell clan member is still remembered as a martyr to this day, even though he was executed well over 300 years ago. James Mitchell was a Covenanter, who featured in one of Scotland's most notorious court cases. The Covenanters were Scots who would not accept that King Charles I was head of the church. They signed a covenant which stated that only Jesus Christ could hold that position.

King Charles inherited the throne in 1625. His father James VI of Scotland became James I of England in March 1603. At that time Scotland and England operated like two distinct countries ruled by the same monarch. They each had their own separate parliament, church, law courts and tax-raising powers. They could even go their own way on foreign policy. Outside the Highlands, where many retained their Catholic convictions, Scotland's religion was Presbyterianism, a harsh strict form of Protestantism. King James believed that his rule had a higher authority than the church's. Despite that he failed in his attempts to force the Scots to embrace his Episcopalian doctrine, which allowed the monarch to appoint bishops to the church.

King Charles, who was born in Fife, decided to finish his father's job and bring the Scots into line. It took him 12 years but in 1637 he ordered that the Book of Common Prayer should be read in St Giles Cathedral, Edinburgh. The congregation was furious. Many believed it was closer to Catholicism than Protestantism.

Hostility to Charles continued to grow and seven months later, in February 1638,

Scotland's National Covenant was published. This document, prepared with the full support of the nobility and land-owning class, proclaimed Scotland's opposition to the king's new prayer book. It was put on public view in Edinburgh and immediately attracted 60,000 signatures. Copies were taken throughout the country and many more signed up.

In 1642 the First English Civil War erupted, between Charles and the forces loyal to his former Parliament, which he had tried to dismiss. The Covenanters allied themselves with the Parliamentarians, known as the Roundheads, who were led by Oliver Cromwell. By May 1646 The Royalists were defeated and Charles surrendered to the Scots. While imprisoned north of the Border he convinced the Covenanters to switch their allegiance to him in return for a promise to make England a Presbyterian state. Soon after, the Covenanters invaded England in the hope of restoring Charles to the throne. This was the start of the Second English Civil War. But they were no match for Cromwell's battle-hardened New

Model Army and were heavily defeated after a series of battles. When the dust settled Charles was executed by public beheading in January 1649 and Cromwell governed the country.

During that time, the Covenanters were split into two camps. The more hard-line Protesters and the more moderate Resolutioners. This latter group were led by James Sharp, who was born in 1613 in Banffshire. He was a graduate of Aberdeen University and became a Presbyterian minister. In 1657 Sharp was sent to London to represent the interests of the Resolutioners. While there, he began to distance himself from his former comrades and began to subscribe to episcopacy, the attempted imposition of which led to the formation of the Covenanters in the first place. In 1660 the Monarchy was restored and King Charles II was welcomed back to England from exile on the Continent. A year later Sharp was appointed Archbishop of St Andrews and immediately began a drive to bring episcopacy to Scotland coupled with a brutal repression of Presbyterianism. This betrayal of his former friends and associates led to a furious reaction from the Covenanters and James Mitchell vowed vengeance. He acquired two pistols and on July 11, 1668 as Archbishop Sharp sat in his coach in Edinburgh's High Street, Mitchell fired his shots at him. Unfortunately for him, and the Covenanters in general, he missed. His bullets hit and wounded Andrew Honeyman, the Bishop of Orkney who was sitting alongside Sharp, in the wrist. In the confusion which followed Mitchell slipped into a nearby house, changed his coat and wig, then stepped back out and joined the noisy crowd. It's thought that many onlookers knew the identity of the would-be assassin but kept quiet because of their hatred for Sharp. It took six years, but eventually the authorities tracked Mitchell down. In January 1676 it was decided that Mitchell should be tortured until he confessed. But he refused to crack and was imprisoned in the notorious Bass Rock, an island prison just off the coast of North Berwick. On December 6, 1677 Mitchell went on trial in Edinburgh where, under the influence of

Archbishop Sharp, he was found guilty and executed the following year. His prosecution had lasted over two years and he had made six appearances in court in what was described as one of Scottish legal history's darkest hours. Sharp, meanwhile, would soon pay for his duplicity. On May 3, 1679 a Covenanter gang attacked him near St Andrews and killed him. As he lay dying they announced that they were avenging the death of James Mitchell.

Over the centuries the Mitchells spread their wings and are now found in every corner of the globe. The name has evolved during that time and it's thought the following may at one time have been related: Mitchell; Mitchal; Mitchel; Mitchelson; Mitchellson; Michell; Michael; Michaels; Michaelson; Michie; Michieson; MacMichie; MacMichy; MacMichael and Carmichael. However, Mitchell remains by far the most popular of that list and, as we will see, clan members have made a remarkable lasting contribution to our life in various parts of the world.

Chapter three:

Great and good

Stephen Mitchell was born in 1789, at Linlithgow, which was the home of the family's tobacco manufacturing plant. It had been set up 66 years earlier by his great grandfather, also Stephen Mitchell. The business passed down from father to son, who all shared the same name.

Stephen Mitchell the fifth took over the reins in 1820. Five years later, as a result of a ban on imports of tobacco at the nearby port of Blackness, Mitchell moved the company to Glasgow. The business continued to grow from strength to strength and in 1859 Mitchell retired to live in Moffat, where he died in 1874 after an accidental fall. Throughout his life Stephen Mitchell was a bit of a loner. He was a member of the Church of Scotland and travelled widely through France and Germany. In his will he left nearly £70,000 to be used to build and maintain a public library in Glasgow. His trustees specified the following conditions to the bequest: That the library was to be known as The Mitchell Library; that the amount of the bequest was to be allowed to remain at interest until it amounted to £70,000, or if thought necessary a larger sum, before a commencement was made; that in the selection of books to form the library, no books should be excluded on the ground that they contravene present opinions on politics or religion; that the library should be freely open to the public under suitable regulations; that contributions of money or of books might be accepted; and that collections of books might be kept together and known by the donor's or other distinctive name. Today the Mitchell Library houses the largest public reference collection in Europe, with 1,213,000 volumes. It also has a substantial lending facility which began in 2005. Meanwhile, the family tobacco business continued to prosper. In 1901, facing increasing competition from the United States, Stephen Mitchell and Son amalgamated with WD & HO

Wills, the Bristol-based market leaders at the time. Eleven other firms joined them, including John Player and Son of Nottingham, to form the Imperial Tobacco Company. A year later Imperial joined forces with their American competitors, the American Tobacco Company, to form the British-American Tobacco Company. Nine years later the Americans withdrew from the partnership but Imperial maintained its stake in BAT until 1980. By then it was known as the Imperial Group Ltd and it controlled a wide range of other businesses, including restaurants, food services and distribution. In 1986 it was sold to the Hanson Trust for £2.5 billion. This may have seemed a great deal of money at the time, but in reality it was a very shrewd piece of business by Hanson. The new owners sold most of the company for £2.3 billion but kept the hugely-profitable tobacco business. The whole deal had cost Hanson a pittance. Today Imperial Tobacco has dozens of plants around the world employing nearly 15,000 people. In 2006 it made a profit before tax of £1.168 billion.

At roughly the same time, at the other end of the world from Glasgow, another Mitchell was responsible for setting up a major public library. Amazingly, he, too, left £70,000 to pay for the project!

James Mitchell had been born in Fife, the son of a farmer, in 1792, just three years after Stephen Mitchell. At the age of 18 he joined the Army Medical Corps and two years later, in April 1812, qualified as a licentiate of the Royal College of Surgeons at Edinburgh. This allowed him to practice medicine. James Mitchell's military career took him to Spain, the USA and the Netherlands. During the Battle of Waterloo in 1815, which ended Napoleon's rule of France, he was stationed at the British military hospital in Brussels. Five years later he was appointed assistant surgeon to the 48th regiment based in Sydney. He resigned from the Army in 1833 and set up a private practice at the same time as running Sydney Hospital. In 1841, after a series of disagreements with the authorities, he resigned from the hospital and began to turn his attention to cultivating large plots of land in which he'd invested. The area is known today as The Hunter Valley, one of Australia's best wine producing regions. As time passed Mitchell became more and more involved in business ventures. It wasn't all plain sailing, though. A fire at a tweed factory in 1851 cost him £25,000. He was also a director of and majority shareholder in the Bank of Australia which lost hundreds of thousands of pounds during the depression of the 1840s. In 1865 Mitchell befriended William Ernest Wolfskehl, who later turned out to be a conman. Wolfskehl convinced Mitchell to back him in a couple of business deals which went spectacularly wrong. Mitchell's family were growing increasingly concerned about the friendship and their fears were confirmed when he died in 1869 and shocked them all by leaving a will naming Wolfskehl as his sole executor. The family contested the will in court and eventually won.

Dr James Mitchell had just one child, David Scott Mitchell who was born in 1836.

David Scott Mitchell was a graduate of the University of Sydney and although called to the Bar did not practise. Instead, he threw himself into the running of the family business in the Hunter River Estates. Although he was a good cricketer, dancer and enjoyed a game of cards, he was a sensitive sort. When his parents died he became a recluse and began devoting a large part of his life to collecting books. He specialised in early Australian editions and manuscripts and by 1900 he had amassed around 10,000 volumes. Mitchell wanted the Australian nation to enjoy his great collection and eventually he bequeathed it to Sydney's public library on condition the authorities built suitable premises. When he died in 1907 he left not only his books but also £70,000 to maintain and expand the collection, which became known as the Mitchell Library, Sydney. When it opened in 1910 it housed 60,000 volumes and is still regarded as one of the world's greatest collections.

Charles Mitchell, who was born in 1820 in Aberdeen, more than left his mark on British shipbuilding. He received his education at schools in his native city and Aberdeen University. While there is no record of his graduation it does not mean he did not complete the course. Many students attended all their classes without going through the graduation ceremony in those days. In 1842, having completed his engineering apprenticeship, he joined another Aberdonian named Coutts who was running a shipyard on the River Tyne. The partnership lasted just two years and in 1844 Mitchell went to London, which would be his home for the next few years. There he worked for Maudsley Son and Fields, one of the world's best-known shipbuilders at the time. Although his career had taken off in London he decided to return to the Tyne after just eight years and set up his own shipbuilding business on the river. This venture was a great success. Between 1853 and 1882 Mitchell's yard completed 450 ships, more than 15 a year! Despite running a booming business he found time for romance and married Anne, the daughter of William Swan.

Their son Charles William Mitchell did not follow in his father's footsteps, but became an artist of some renown.

In the 1860s Charles Senior was called to St Petersburg where he oversaw the setting up of new shipyards for the Russian authorities. He left a relative in charge of the yard and under his guidance the firm completed several armoured vessels in conjunction with another nearby firm run by Sir William Armstrong. In 1882 the two companies became partners employing upwards of 15,000. They were known as Sir WG Armstrong Mitchell and Company and quickly established a worldwide reputation for building warships, but their most important creation at the time was the Gluckauf, now regarded as the world's first oil tanker. As Charles began to take a backseat in the business he turned his attention to philanthropy.

He funded the construction of St George's Church in Jesmond, and provided substantial sums to Aberdeen University who named the tower in Marischall College after him.

In addition they named the graduation hall the Mitchell Hall in his honour. He died in 1895. Two years later, Sir WG Armstrong Mitchell and Co. merged with Sir Joseph Whitworth and Co. and with no member of the Mitchell family on the board, the name was quietly dropped and the new company was registered as Armstrong Whitworth and Co Ltd.

While all this had been happening, Charles Mitchell played a major role in another shipbuilding enterprise on the Tyne. This company, which ultimately became famous as Swan Hunter, rose from an inauspicious start to become a giant of the industry. After his marriage, Charles took on his two brothers-in-law, Harry Frederick and Charles Sheridan Swan. Things went well for the trio and soon they were looking for bigger premises, where they could set up a subsidiary. They found them in 1873 in Wallsend. Just 12 months later this new enterprise faced financial troubles and Charles Mitchell was forced to take a more hands on approach. However, there were so many demands on his time, he was forced to leave the day-to-day running to Charles Sheridan Swan. Unfortunately he died in an accident in 1879 and shortly after Mitchell was approached by another shipbuilder with a big reputation. His name was George Burton Hunter and the new company Swan Hunter was born, with Hunter as managing director. It is still in existence to this day.

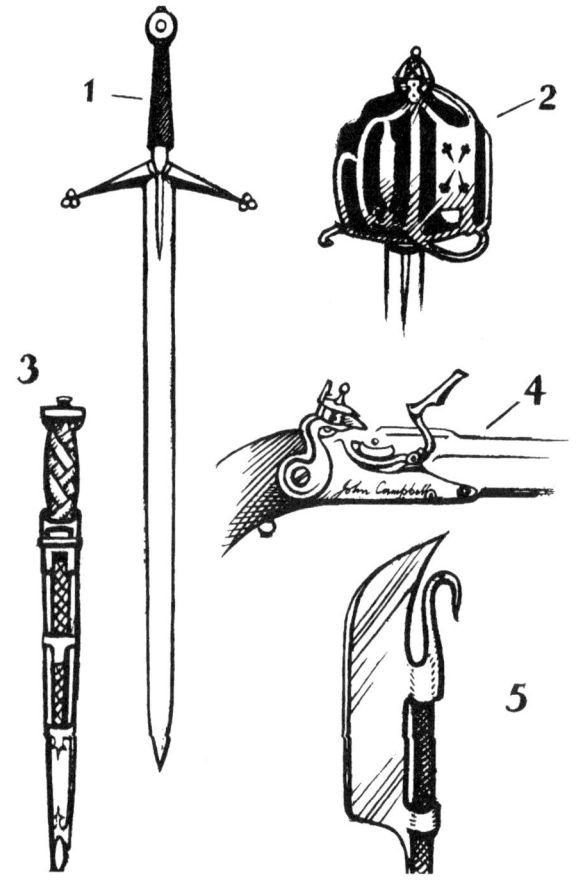

Highland weapons

1)   The claymore or two-handed sword
        (fifteenth or early sixteenth century)

2)   Basket hilt of broadsword
        made in Stirling, 1716

3)   Highland dirk
        (eighteenth century)

4)   Steel pistol *(detail)* made in Doune

5)   Head of Lochaber Axe as carried
        in the '45 and earlier